fresh
in autumn

fresh
in autumn

RYLAND
PETERS
& SMALL

cooking with Alastair Hendy

photography by David Loftus

First published in Great Britain in 1999
by Ryland Peters & Small
Cavendish House, 51–55 Mortimer Street,
London W1N 7TD

Printed and bound in China
by Toppan Printing Co.

ISBN 1 900518 85 6

A CIP record for this book is available from the
British Library

Acknowledgements
My thanks to Egg, of Kinnerton Street, Belgravia,
London, who were so generous in lending
beautiful bowls for photography, to Kara Kara,
Pond Place, South Kensington, London, for
Japanese table mats and utensils, to Ulrika at
Alma Home, Greatorex Street, Shoreditch in
London for woven leather runners, and cashmere
and suede throws, to Panzers of St John's Wood,
London, for the fresh produce, and to Priscilla and
Antonio Carluccio of Carluccio's Restaurant in
London for the mushrooms and truly wild funghi.

Notes
Cooking and eating wrongly identified mushrooms
can be fatal. If in doubt, don't.
Neither the author nor the publishers can ever
accept any legal responsibility or liability for any
errors, omissions or mistaken identification of
fungus species that may be made.
All spoon measurements are level unless
otherwise noted.
Specialist Asian ingredients are available in large
supermarkets, Thai, Chinese, Japanese and
Vietnamese shops, as well as Asian stores.

Designer
Robin Rout
Food Editor
Elsa Petersen-Schepelern
Editorial Assistant
Maddalena Bastianelli
Production
Patricia Harrington
Head of Design
Gabriella Le Grazie
Publishing Director
Anne Ryland

Food Stylist
Alastair Hendy
Cooking Assistant
Kate Habershon
Stylist
Alastair Hendy
Author Photograph
David Loftus

Dedication

To my mother

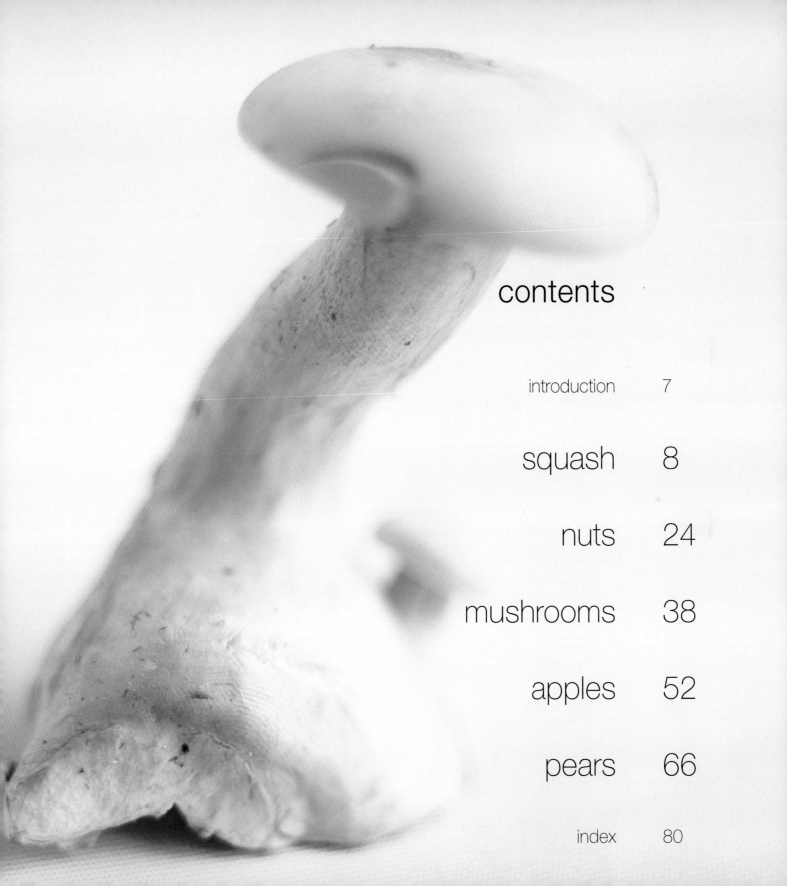

contents

To me, autumn means the fruits of the field, orchard and forest; pumpkins of all shapes and hides; fresh nuts; a complete compendium of mushrooms; bags of apples and pears. It means slow-cooked stews with layers of flavour; braises, bakes and roasts, and a full quota of comfortable puddings.

This book is for everyone – cooks and non-cooks, for those who are just starting and for those who like others to cook for them. If you're not an accomplished cook or haven't had much practice, just follow the recipe and all should be well. It's how I learned to cook – from books. My mother spent time in the kitchen cooking for the family but wasn't always too keen on engaging eager-to-help little hands. If I offered to cook supper she'd happily stay clear – offering advice from afar – from her bath. I was forever being told to look it up in 'the book' (which book I was never quite sure). So I now know how important it is for a recipe to be accurate, so that it works and tastes good. My mother's canny 'tuition' was spot-on.

Fresh in Autumn has short quick recipes for when you want instant satisfaction – and others that will need time in the oven and, for some, a well-earned snooze on the sofa. It's for everyone who loves food. And for those who dream of a picture-perfect season of so-called mellow fruitfulness, the gentle warmth of the oven with its promise of dinner, steamy windows and pot-roast aromas. Perfect.

Squash don't look real. They don't look like food either. Outrageously shaped, knobbled and gnarled, they look positively extra-terrestrial. Some, like acorn squash, look like grenades, butternut squash defy description, whereas the big jolly orange ones are most at home when etched with a big toothy cartoon grin – with names like Hubbard, Turk's Cap and Munchkins. With hides like old leather, they are the true eccentrics of the vegetable patch.

Inside they are tender and sweet. The flesh is dense yet delicate when cooked; bold in flavour and colour – yet sensuous and light. Don't just relegate them to a decorative role – they are the edible stars of autumn.

Pumpkins, marrows, courgettes, custard marrows, Chinese winter melons, pattypan and other squash (of which their are hundreds of varieties) all belong to the *Cucurbita* genus of edible gourds. In this book, I've used the varieties that are at their best in autumn. Marrows, courgettes and others with edible skins belong to the summer kitchen. Butternut and acorn squash both have excellent flavour and so do the large, lobed varieties with leathery skins – these can usually be bought in more manageable cut portions.

Pumpkins can be baked whole in their skins, roasted in sections, boiled or steamed. Don't be afraid to experiment – pumpkin can handle it. Apart from making soup (one of my favourites – particularly good with fried apple and salty cheese stirred in), and classic American pumpkin pie, you can add it to casseroles, braises and tagines. It's brilliant with spices, or doused with olive oil, flavoured with herbs and roasted alongside onions; thick slices can be baked with butter, then topped with cheese and grilled; steamed nuggets can be stirred into creamy risotto and pasta.

So if you're still one of the unconverted, next time you spot a squash, add him to your shopping basket and try one of these recipes – you'll discover beauty's much more than (knobbly) skin deep.

squash

Pumpkin soup

with Creole roasted pumpkin seeds and ash-crust goat's cheese

A bowl of hot pumpkin soup on a cold, wet, autumn day – just add a slice or three of goats' cheese and a good sprinkling of crisp pumpkin seeds and your soup will turn into a meal. Use dense-fleshed pumpkin with brown, grey or dark green skins – orange-skinned varieties tend to be watery.

1.5 kg pumpkin, halved and peeled

olive oil, for frying and baking

1 onion, finely chopped

2 garlic cloves, crushed

2 teaspoons cumin seeds, toasted

2 sprigs of thyme

2 bay leaves

½ teaspoon freshly grated nutmeg

1 teaspoon ground allspice

1.5 litres chicken stock

salt and freshly ground black pepper

1 ash-crust goats' cheese log
or 1 small tub of goats' curd cheese
to serve

Creole roasted pumpkin seeds:

2 teaspoons olive oil

½ teaspoon garlic salt

½ teaspoon onion powder

1 teaspoon paprika

a pinch of cayenne

1 teaspoon dried oregano

Serves 4

1

Remove and reserve the pumpkin seeds. Cut the pumpkin flesh into large chunks.

2

Heat 2 tablespoons olive oil in a deep frying pan, add the onion and garlic and fry until soft. Add salt and pepper, the cumin seeds, thyme, bay leaves, nutmeg and allspice. Fry for 1 minute. Add the stock and pumpkin and simmer gently for about 30 minutes or until soft. Purée in a food processor, transfer to a saucepan and keep it warm.

3

Clean the fibres off the pumpkin seeds, then toss the seeds with the olive oil, garlic salt, onion powder, paprika, cayenne and oregano. Spread over a baking sheet and roast in a preheated oven at 200°C (400°F) Gas 6 for 10–15 minutes.

4

Serve the soup accompanied by the toasted seeds and slices of goats' cheese.

Variations:
• Replace the toasted pumpkin seeds with fried crispy sage leaves.
• Use freshly grated Parmesan or Gruyère instead of goats' cheese.

Pumpkin fondue with artichokes and sage

A hybrid dish – a mixture of Swiss fondue, pumpkin soup, plus classic New Orleans artichoke and cheese dip. And it's sublime. The baked pumpkin and runny cheese flavoured with sage and artichokes are magic together. Dip in with breadsticks and scoop out the pumpkin with spoons – make sure your friends are well acquainted with each other, this is communal dining.

1 medium flat pumpkin (such as Crown Prince, pictured)

½ teaspoon freshly grated nutmeg

60 g butter

1 onion, very finely chopped

1 garlic clove, crushed

150 ml dry white wine

1 teaspoon plain flour

5 sprigs of sage, chopped

2 teaspoons dried oregano

4 baby artichokes in oil, drained and chopped

600 g Emmental or Gruyère cheese (or a mixture), grated

100 ml sour cream

salt and freshly ground black pepper

green Tabasco, to taste (optional)

Caraway bread sticks:

500 g packet ciabatta bread mix

1 tablespoon dried oregano

1 tablespoon caraway seeds

olive oil, for greasing

melted butter, for brushing

semolina flour, for dusting

Serves 4

1

To make the bread sticks, follow the packet instructions to the first rising of the dough, then divide in half. Add the oregano to one half and the caraway seeds to the other, and knead again. Roll out each piece to 5 mm thick and slice into 2 cm wide strips. Put, spaced apart, on a baking sheet greased with olive oil and let rise in a warm place for 10 minutes. Brush with melted butter, dust with semolina flour and bake in a preheated oven at 230°C (450°F) Gas 8 for 15 minutes or until golden brown.

2

Slice the top off the pumpkin and reserve it, hollow out the core and discard all the fibres and seeds. Rub with salt, pepper and nutmeg, and smear the inside with half the butter. Put into a roasting tin and bake in a preheated oven at 180°C (350°F) Gas 4 for 45 minutes to 1 hour, or until almost cooked.

3

Heat the remaining butter in a frying pan, add the onion and garlic and sauté until soft and translucent. Add the wine, heat to simmering, then add all the remaining ingredients, except the sour cream, and stir until the cheese melts.

4

Spoon the cheese mixture into the pumpkin, stir in the sour cream, replace the lid, and continue baking for about 20 minutes. Serve with bread sticks and spoons.

Acorn squash with ginger and seaweed

Acorn squash has dense golden flesh. It's a little difficult to peel as it is so deeply ribbed – cutting it up first then peeling the wedges is the best way to tackle it. It suits these Japanese flavours and is especially good with grated fresh ginger. Add noodles and you have a complete meal.

3 bundles somen or udon noodles (optional)

25 g dried hijiki or wakame seaweed*

1 small acorn squash, about 750 g

500 ml dashi (use instant dashi and follow the packet instructions)*

3 tablespoons mirin (sweetened rice wine)*

1 tablespoon sugar

4 tablespoons light soy sauce

3 cm fresh ginger, finely sliced and shredded, to serve

Serves 4

Note: Seaweed, dashi and mirin are sold in Asian markets, and often available in larger supermarkets.

1

Cook the somen noodles, if using, for about 2 minutes in boiling water until *al dente*. Rinse in cold water, drain, then let return to room temperature.

2

Put the seaweed into a bowl of cold water until soft and rehydrated. Drain.

3

Cut the squash into quarters, deseed, peel, slice each piece in half crossways, then again lengthways.

4

Put the squash into a saucepan, add the dashi, mirin, sugar and soy sauce, bring to the boil, then simmer for 15 minutes. Add the drained seaweed and warm through for 1 minute.

5

Divide the noodles between 4 bowls, add the squash, seaweed and a ladle of hot flavoured stock. Top with shredded ginger, or serve separately, so people can help themselves.

Variations:

• Instead of seaweed add finely shredded spring onion or stems of watercress.

Pumpkin coconut curry

Make this curry with ordinary pumpkin, or with spaghetti squash – melon-shaped, with yellow flesh that pulls into strands when cooked. I prefer to bake it first before adding to the curry, to retain the long strands.

500 g spaghetti squash or pumpkin, peeled, deseeded and cut into chunks

10 small shallots, finely sliced lengthways

4 garlic cloves, crushed

½ teaspoon turmeric

3 cm fresh ginger, chopped

2 stalks lemongrass, finely chopped

1 tablespoon red Thai curry paste

3 tablespoons salted cashew nuts

4 tablespoons peanut oil, plus extra for brushing

1 teaspoon tamarind paste
or 1 tablespoon fresh lemon juice

400 ml canned coconut milk

200 ml chicken or vegetable stock

salt

to serve:

fresh coriander leaves

fresh beansprouts

Serves 4

1

If using spaghetti squash, brush it with a little oil and salt, then bake in a preheated oven at 190°C (375°F) Gas 5 for 30–45 minutes until cooked. Pull the flesh into strings. If using regular pumpkin, cut it into bite-sized chunks.

2

Place 4 shallots, the garlic, turmeric, ginger, lemongrass, Thai curry paste and cashew nuts into an electric blender and process to a coarse paste.

3

Heat 2 tablespoons of the oil in a frying pan, add the paste and fry until it darkens, adding a drop more oil if required. Add the tamarind or lemon juice, pumpkin or squash, coconut milk and stock and simmer for 10 minutes or until the pumpkin is tender.

4

Heat the remaining oil in a second pan, add the remaining shallots and fry until crisp. Spread out on kitchen paper to drain. Sprinkle liberally with salt.

5

Divide the pumpkin or squash between 4 bowls and serve topped with fried shallots, coriander and beansprouts.

Chinatown pumpkin

Dropping in to my local Chinatown for a bundle of bok choy, I can't help but leave with an extra bag, full of weird dried ingredients. This recipe will, for some of us, charter unknown territory, but don't let that put you off. The shopping is easy (everything can be bought from a Chinese food shop) it's easy to make and delicious. It's Chinatown packed into a pumpkin.

6 dried shiitake mushrooms

8 dried oriental black fungus (optional)

1 tablespoon dried shrimp (optional)

300 ml glutinous rice, soaked overnight in a bowl of water

2 dried Chinese sausages

500 g cooked Chinese crispy duck and/or pork, sliced and boned

1 tablespoon light soy sauce

sesame oil

6 white custard marrows*

1 teaspoon five-spice powder

salt

To serve:

chilli oil

soy sauce

Serves 6

Note and variation:

This recipe is also illustrated on page 2, using Little Gem squash, peeled then stuffed as in the main recipe. They were then gently poached for 25 minutes in a covered saucepan with 1 litre chicken stock, 3 tablespoons rice wine, 4 cm sliced fresh ginger, and 4 halved spring onions. They were served in a pool of poaching juices.

1

Put the mushrooms, fungus and shrimp, if using, in a bowl with cold water to cover. Soak for 30 minutes or until rehydrated. Drain.

2

Line a Chinese steamer with muslin or tea towel. Drain the rice and spread it over the muslin, put the Chinese sausages on top, and steam over boiling water for 25 minutes, topping up with extra boiling water if necessary. (The rice will be sticky.)

3

Slice the sausage and mix with the rice, mushrooms, duck and/or pork and shrimp, if using. Season with soy sauce and sesame oil.

4

Cut the tops off the custard marrows, remove the core and seeds and rub the flesh with five-spice powder and salt. Stuff the rice mixture into the squash, replace the cap, put into the steamer and steam for about 40 minutes or until the squash is cooked (test with the point of a knife).

5

Serve with chilli oil and soy sauce.

Grilled chicken

and pumpkin couscous with honey, mint and cardamom lemon oil

Don't be put off by the long list of ingredients – though there are many different spices, they are all quite ordinary things by today's standards and you probably have them in your cupboard already.

150 ml olive oil

20 cardamom pods, crushed

1 large whole lemon, coarsely chopped

4 chicken breast fillets

1 butternut squash, halved, deseeded and thickly sliced

1½ chicken stock cubes

300 g couscous

torn leaves from 1 bunch of mint, plus extra to serve

a bunch of chives, finely chopped

2 red onions, halved and finely sliced

2 garlic cloves, crushed

1 teaspoon ground cumin

1 teaspoon ground coriander

½ teaspoon ground cinnamon

a pinch of saffron (optional)

2 teaspoons clear honey

1 tablespoon pine nuts

sea salt and freshly ground black pepper

Serves 4

1

Put the oil, cardamom pods and lemon in a small frying pan and heat gently (do not fry) until the lemon peel is lightly stewed and softened. Let cool.

2

Season the chicken and squash and rub with some of the cardamom lemon oil. Preheat a stove-top grill pan (ridged, if you want black lines), add the chicken and squash and cook for 2–3 minutes on each side.

3

Dissolve the stock cubes in 1 litre boiling water. Put the couscous in a bowl and pour over enough stock to just cover (don't be tempted to add more stock). Season and leave to swell. Fluff through with a fork after 5 minutes. Stir in the mint and chives.

4

Heat 1 tablespoon of the oil in a large shallow saucepan, add the onions, garlic and ground spices and fry until the onions are soft. Add the saffron, if using, honey, pine nuts and remaining stock. Season lightly. Add the pumpkin, put the chicken on top, and heat to simmering. Partly cover the pan with a lid, then cook for about 10 minutes until the squash is just soft.

4

Divide the couscous between 4 bowls, add the spiced onion, chicken (sliced if you wish) and squash, pour over the hot juices, then serve topped with a few extra mint leaves..

Variations:
• Instead of chicken use roast duck confit (page 54).
• Use cardamom lemon oil to brush meat or vegetables before grilling or roasting.

Lamb shanks
with autumn squash ratatouille

Lamb shank is the upper foreleg of the animal. Allow for 3 hours of slow braising – this one can't be rushed. In fact the shanks taste better if cooked the day before (until stage 3) and left to saturate and cool in their juices; the final result is meat that is meltingly tender and falls from the bone.

4 lamb shanks, trimmed

3 garlic cloves, cut into slivers

2 tablespoons olive oil, for frying, plus extra, for brushing

1 large onion, finely chopped

1 large carrot, finely chopped

2 sticks celery, finely chopped

2 tablespoons tomato paste

3 bay leaves

2 strips orange peel

200 ml white wine

2 red peppers, deseeded and sliced, or 2 Italian sun-dried red peppers*

1 small butternut or acorn squash, halved lengthways, peeled, deseeded and sliced

1 tablespoon capers

150 g black olives, pitted if preferred

small bunch basil, leaves only

sea salt and freshly ground black pepper

Serves 4

From Italian delicatessens.

1
Season the lamb and stab all over with a knife. Insert the garlic slivers into the incisions. Heat 1 tablespoon of the oil in a large, heavy-based frying pan. Brush each shank with olive oil, add to the pan in batches and fry until brown on all sides. Remove and set aside. Add the remaining oil to the pan and heat gently.

2
Add the onion, carrot and celery and fry until browned. Mix in the tomato paste, bay leaves, orange peel and seasoning. Cook for 2 minutes. Add the wine and 200 ml water, bring to the boil then simmer until reduced by half. Transfer to a small, deep roasting tin.

3
Add the lamb shanks, cover tightly with foil and cook in a preheated oven at 150°C (300°F) Gas 3 for 2 hours.

4
Heat the remaining oil in the frying pan. Brush the peppers with olive oil and season with salt and freshly ground black pepper. Add to the pan and cook until lightly browned on both sides. Add to the lamb shanks, then add the squash, capers, olives and a little extra water if necessary. Continue braising for 1 hour or until the squash is tender.

5
Remove from the oven, then top with the basil leaves and serve with creamy mashed potato or crusty bread.

There's an art to cracking a nut. The conventional nutcracker, for me, is not up to it. The metal grippers splinter the edible part of the nut everywhere. I'm always left with a few meagre scraps of kernel held firmly between feisty pieces of shell hanging on for dear life, and shell scraps all over the table and floor.

I can manage hazelnuts, which always seem to come out whole, but maybe everyone has their favourite nut, one that performs and behaves for them (one person's walnut heaven is another's walnut hell).

Screw-mechanism nut crackers are pretty accurate: designed for perfect crack control, a bit like a thumbscrew, they stop your nuts from flying everywhere. Now let's be serious: the best way to crack nuts is not with any man-made device, but with a simple stone. Not your usual handy kitchen or table utensil, I know, but it works (for me) and I keep a rounded stone for this purpose (plus other culinary purposes too). All you need is a gentle, centralized tap and the nut usually opens precisely, with minimum splinter velocity. It's perfect.

Nuts are eaten throughout the world – before, during and after meals – salted, toasted, dry roasted, fried, spiced or plain, simply cracked (don't you believe it) from the shell. They are a world staple and are used in many cooked dishes: sauces, stuffings, curries, tart cases and pastries are thickened and packed with ground or whole nuts. Each region has its favourites; in Britain it's hazelnuts and chestnuts; in Spain, it's chiefly almonds; Italy – pine nuts; Africa – peanuts; the Middle East – almonds, pine nuts and pistachios; India – almonds and cashews; South-east Asia – coconuts and candlenuts; and America – pecans.

Nuts are protein-rich, full of vitamins, calcium, iron and oils (and calories, too, unfortunately). Because of their high oil content they should not be stored for too long or in too warm conditions – the resinous oil can turn rancid. So buy them as you need them and make a point of enjoying them in autumn when they're in season, for then they're sweet and milky. My favourites for cooking are hazelnuts and cob nuts, roasted, skinned and baked into a crisp meringue or cake – they are the toasty scent of autumn. Thank God they're the easiest to crack.

nuts

Spice island dumplings

The spice islands of Indonesia still retain their plantations of nutmeg, clove, cinnamon and nuts. I dreamt up this recipe while sitting on top of an island volcano, looking over the spice groves below. It contains all the flavours of Indonesia in a nut dumpling, simply prepared and cooked.

1.5 litres light chicken stock

2 stalks lemongrass, trimmed and smashed

8 kaffir lime leaves, torn,
or the juice of ½ lime, plus 1 teaspoon sugar

2 garlic cloves, thickly sliced

3 cm fresh ginger, thickly sliced

1 packet rice vermicelli noodles, about 30 g, soaked in hot water for 4 minutes, drained and rinsed

Chinese leaves, such as bok choy

Spice dumplings:

250 g peeled prawns, fresh or frozen and thawed

250 g pork mince

3 cm fresh ginger, peeled and finely grated

2 tablespoons finely chopped coriander

60 g canned bamboo shoots, drained

16 macadamia nuts

4 spring onions, trimmed and chopped

2 small red chillies, finely chopped

½ tablespoon *kecap manis* or dark soy sauce

1 tablespoon fish sauce or 1 teaspoon salt

2 tablespoons lime juice

a pinch of ground cloves

a pinch of ground cinnamon

1 small egg, lightly beaten, to bind

vegetable oil, for frying

Serves 4

1

Put the chicken stock, lemongrass, lime leaves or juice and sugar, garlic and ginger in a saucepan, bring to the boil and simmer, covered, for about 20 minutes. Taste and add salt if necessary. Strain into a clean pan and discard the flavourings.

2

To make the dumplings, put the prawns in a food processor and chop for 1–2 seconds. Transfer to a bowl. Add all the remaining ingredients except the egg and oil to the processor and work to a coarse crumb consistency. Mix with the prawns and egg. Roll the mixture into walnut-sized balls and chill for 30 minutes.

3

Heat the vegetable oil in a frying pan or deep-fryer, add the dumplings in batches and cook gently until golden brown all over, about 2–3 minutes. Remove and set aside.

4

To serve, reheat the broth and arrange a portion of noodles and a few leaves in 4 deep soup bowls. Divide the dumplings between the bowls and pour over the hot lime broth.

Variations:

• Use Brazil nuts instead of macadamia nuts.
• Spear each dumpling with a bamboo skewer, fry and serve with drinks.

Persian chicken with coconut and pistachios

Coconut is one of the most delicious of all nuts – and thankfully it is available all year round. Almonds and pistachios are typical of Persian and Moghul cooking, prized for their colour as well as flavour. The curry improves with time, so try to make it the day before.

4 free-range chicken legs, skinned and cut into thigh and drumstick portions

¼ teaspoon ground cinnamon

¼ teaspoon ground cloves

6 tablespoons sunflower oil

6 garlic cloves, chopped

3 cm fresh ginger, chopped

5 tablespoons blanched whole almonds

2 onions, chopped

4 dried chillies

6 black cardamom pods, bruised

4 teaspoons garam masala

6 tablespoons creamy Greek yoghurt

250 ml canned coconut milk

2 tablespoons sultanas

salt

To serve:

finely grated flesh of ½ fresh coconut

1 tablespoon slivered nuts, such as almonds and pistachios

4 small bananas, such as apple bananas, peeled and sliced (optional)

Serves 4

Note: *The whole chillies and cardamoms are for flavouring only – tell your guests not to eat them.*

1

Rub the chicken pieces with the cinnamon, cloves and a little salt. Heat the oil in a non-stick frying pan, add the chicken and fry on all sides until golden. Transfer to a flameproof casserole. Retain the oil in the pan.

2

Put the garlic, ginger, almonds and onions in a food processor and work to a paste, adding a drop of water if necessary.

3

Add the chillies and black cardamom pods to the oil and fry until the chillies blister. Add the onion mixture and garam masala and fry until the paste darkens – keep stirring to avoid burning. Strain off excess oil.

4

Slowly stir in the yoghurt, 1 tablespoon at a time, then stir in the coconut milk, 100 ml water and the sultanas. Pour around the chicken in the casserole and heat to simmering. Cook, covered, in a preheated oven at 160°C (300°F) Gas 2 for 1 hour.

5

Serve topped with grated coconut, slivered nuts and banana, if using.

Beef stew with chestnuts

You have to have patience to prepare and peel fresh chestnuts – it's a real fiddle. However you can now buy stress-free, vacuum-packed chestnuts, which have been peeled and part-cooked – they taste good and take all the hard work out of chestnut preparation.

1.5 kg blade or stewing steak, cut into 4 pieces*

3½ tablespoons beef dripping or olive oil

1 large onion, finely chopped

2 garlic cloves, crushed

2 bay leaves

1 star anise (optional)

2 carrots, finely chopped

2 celery stalks, finely chopped

1 tablespoon tomato purée

1½ bottles red wine

18 chestnuts

1 teaspoon sugar

salt and freshly ground black pepper

Serves 6–8

1

Rub the meat with salt and plenty of pepper. Heat a heavy, flameproof casserole until hot, add 2 tablespoons dripping or oil and add the meat. Leave without moving until well browned and caramelized, about 2 minutes. Turn over and continue browning until all sides are done. Remove from the casserole.

2

Add 1 tablespoon dripping or oil, add the onion, garlic, bay leaves, star anise, if using, carrots and celery and fry until browned. Add salt and pepper, stir in the tomato purée and cook for 1 minute. Add the wine and 300 ml water, bring to the boil, then simmer until reduced by half.

3

Put the meat back into the casserole with the vegetable wine mixture, cover, then let braise gently in a preheated oven at 150°C (300°F) Gas 2 for 3 hours.

4

If using fresh chestnuts, part-slice the chestnut skins open on their curved side, then boil for 5 minutes. Strain, cool, then peel and remove the brown pith. Heat the remaining dripping or oil in a frying pan, add the sugar and chestnuts and fry until caramelized, about 3 minutes. Add to the casserole, then return to the oven to braise for a further 40 minutes. Serve with buttery mashed potato flavoured with mustard or horseradish.

** **Note:** Try to use blade of beef (from the shoulder) for this recipe: it is marbled with fat and connective tissue and especially suited to long, slow cooking. The meat is lubricated as it cooks, becoming moist and tender.*

Pecan pork with apple and maple syrup

Pecans taste like walnuts, but a touch sweeter. You'll need string and bamboo skewers to tie the pork. Remove the string before serving, but leave the skewers in the meat to hold each portion together.

1 loin of pork (about 1.5 kg), trimmed but with skin included

½ teaspoon ground allspice

3 tablespoons olive oil

5 tablespoons maple syrup

30 g butter

6 apples, cored and quartered

salt and freshly ground black pepper

Pecan stuffing:

150 g shelled pecans

1 onion, chopped

2 garlic cloves, crushed

leaves from 1 bunch of flat leaf parsley

1 bunch of sage, stems discarded

100 g fresh breadcrumbs

2 cloves, ground

1 egg, lightly beaten

salt and freshly ground black pepper

Serves 4

1
To make the stuffing, work the nuts in a food processor until finely chopped but not ground. Transfer to a large bowl. Add the onion, garlic and herbs to the processor and chop finely.

2
Heat 2 tablespoons olive oil in a frying pan, add the onion mixture and cook gently until softened. Stir into the pecan mixture, then stir in the ground cloves, salt, pepper and egg. Open up the natural cavity in the joint and stuff with the pecan stuffing. Close up and tie the length of the loin with string.

3
Place the meat in a roasting tin. Using a craft knife or very sharp kitchen knife, score the skin and fat with fine parallel slashes. Pierce and secure at regular intervals with bamboo or wooden skewers. Rub with plenty of salt, pepper, allspice and the remaining oil. Roast in a preheated oven at 220°C (425°F) Gas 7 for 30 minutes. Pour over half the maple syrup, lower the heat to 190°C (375°F) Gas 5, then roast for a further 45 minutes.

4
Heat the butter in a frying pan, add the apple quarters and fry until lightly browned. Pour in the remaining maple syrup and cook for about 2 minutes until lightly caramelized. Arrange around the pork for the last 10 minutes of cooking. Remove from the oven and set aside, loosely covered with foil, for 10 minutes before carving. To serve, slice the pork as skewered portions and serve with celeriac or parsnip mash.

Nut fudge shortbread

Caramel squares, found in old-fashioned bakers, cafés and tea shops, are pretty lethal. Sweetly addictive, they will work wonders (but in the wrong direction – to your waistline). Eat one, do eighty press-ups, that's the way to do it. I make mine with nuts and raisins.

300 g plain flour

a pinch of salt

120 g caster sugar

240 g unsalted butter

200 g plump raisins

220 g pecans or walnut halves

200 g dark chocolate

Fudge:

120 g unsalted butter

120 g light muscovado sugar

2 tablespoons golden syrup

170 g sweetened condensed milk (1 small can)

Serves 4

1

To make the shortbread, put the flour, salt, sugar and butter into a food processor and pulse until the pastry forms a ball. Alternatively, using your fingertips, rub the butter into the flour to resemble fine crumbs, then work in the salt and sugar. Press the mixture into a 20 x 30 cm Swiss roll tin and smooth with the back of a knife. Sprinkle with raisins and press flat. Bake in a preheated oven at 180°C (350°F) Gas 4 for 20–25 minutes.

2

Put all the fudge ingredients into a non-stick saucepan and heat gently, but do not boil. Whisk thoroughly together.

3

Line the nuts across the cooked shortbread base, then pour over the hot fudge mixture. Smooth with a palette knife and chill until firm.

4

Melt the chocolate in a heatproof bowl set over a saucepan of gently simmering water. Pour the chocolate over the set fudge mixture, smooth with a palette knife and leave to set. Cut into slices or fingers before serving.

Hazelnut tiramisu cake

The flavour of hazelnuts and cob nuts is heightened when they're roasted. Shell, then roast for 10 minutes in a moderate oven and rub off the skins with a tea towel.

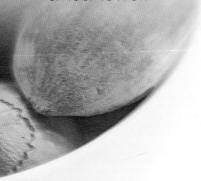

4 eggs

250 g caster sugar

190 g plain flour, sieved

100 g hazelnuts, roasted, skinned and coarsely ground

1 teaspoon vanilla essence

Tiramisu filling:

2 eggs

2 tablespoons caster sugar

650 g mascarpone

250 ml double cream

120 ml strong coffee (cold)

4 tablespoons coffee liqueur, such as Kahlua

cocoa powder, for dusting

Chocolate band casing (optional):*

300 g dark cooking chocolate, broken into pieces

Serves 4

2 round 18-cm springform cake tins, buttered and base-lined with greaseproof paper

1

To make the cake, whisk the eggs with an electric whisk or mixer until frothy. Gradually whisk in the sugar until the mixture is absolutely white and holds its shape. Fold in the flour, hazelnuts and vanilla. Divide the mixture between the 2 buttered cake tins. Bake in a preheated oven at 180°C, (350°F) Gas 4 for 25–30 minutes, or until firm to the touch. Let cool, then remove the paper and slice each sponge into 2 rounds.

2

To make the filling, beat the eggs with the sugar in a large bowl, then beat in the mascarpone. Reserve one-third of the mixture in a small bowl. Beat the cream to soft peak stage and fold into the mixture in the large bowl. Mix the coffee with the coffee liqueur in a cup or jug.

3

To assemble the cake, put a round of sponge on a serving plate and sprinkle with the liqueur coffee mixture. Cover with a thick layer of mascarpone cream. Top with another round of sponge and repeat the process until all the sponge has been used. (Don't sprinkle coffee right to the edges and leave the top sponge unsprinkled.) Using a palette knife, cover the top and the sides of the cake with a layer of the reserved mascarpone. Chill until serving and dust with cocoa powder if you like.

*Note: To make the Chocolate Band Casing, put the chocolate into a heatproof bowl set over a saucepan of simmering water. Melt until smooth and lump-free. Cut out a rectangle of card measuring the outside circumference of the cake tin x height of the cake. Set on a large, smooth work surface. Pour the chocolate over the card, spreading with a palette knife until the edges are covered. Smooth level. Let cool a little but not set. When the chocolate loses its 'gloss', carefully excavate along one short edge of the card, lift up and peel away from the work surface. Bend the chocolate-covered card around the cake (chocolate on the inside) with a small overlapping 'seam' and secure with tape. Refrigerate until set, then remove the tape and carefully peel off the card.

'Mushrooms on toast' – it says it all. It would be my last meal on Earth. It's pure mushroominess, it's autumn, it's the one meal I can never tire of and the simplest mushroom dish of all. But I'm not talking any old mushroom on toast: it has to be either the giant flat-cap field mushrooms or a host of perfect pearly little buttons, preferably plucked fresh from dewy morning turf. Unfortunately it's the cultivated variety that usually reaches my plate. Turf and woods, let alone wild growing mushrooms, are hard to come by in tarmac land. (Though I think I could insist on turf-grown, for my last meal on Earth.)

The good thing about mushrooms is you have to do so little to them. All they need is a gentle brushing to remove any dirt (never wash them), trim off any woody stems, then fry them quickly in butter or olive oil with chopped garlic and seasoning (and possibly a sprinkling of chopped parsley).

Mix them with salad, cooked pasta, rice or potatoes, or embellish them with a poached egg – the possibilities positively mushroom.

Depending on where you live, there can be dozens of cultivated 'wild' funghi to choose from. The most common include oyster mushrooms, which grow in sprouting cascades on dead wood (very pretty, but also pretty tasteless and watery); shiitakes – meaty with a distinct and full wood-smoked flavour; the weird enokii, with their long-stemmed white pinnules, and ceps (porcini), the king of mushrooms with a heady mushroom musk. Other wild mushrooms are often sold fresh in autumn – buy them and try them. However, don't go foraging for wild mushrooms unless you know exactly what you're picking – some are lethal.

rooms

Roasted mushrooms
with horseradish mascarpone

Mushrooms on toast are, for me, the definitive mushroom meal. Simple and straight to the point. Though I don't usually like to muck about with it, this recipe with hot horseradish and thyme still follows the purist path – the combination is wonderful.

6 large open mushrooms, stems removed, caps well brushed

a bunch of thyme

120 g butter, softened, plus extra, for greasing

3 garlic cloves, crushed

6 thick slices white bread, toasted

sea salt and freshly ground black pepper

Horseradish mascarpone:

5 cm fresh horseradish root, peeled and grated, or 2 tablespoons horseradish sauce

200 g mascarpone cheese

Serves 6

1
Thoroughly mix the freshly grated horseradish with the mascarpone and set aside.

2
Put the mushrooms, gills upward, in a greased roasting tin. Sprinkle with sea salt and pepper, and tuck the thyme around them.

3
Mix 90 g of the butter with the garlic and dot over the mushrooms. Roast in a preheated oven at 190ºC (375ºF) Gas 5 for about 10 minutes.

4
Spread the toast with the remaining butter. Add a mushroom and a spoonful of horseradish mascarpone to each slice. Sprinkle with the thyme leaves and serve.

Porcini pizza with garlic butter

Porcini – 'little pigs' in Italian – are also known as ceps and are the kings of the mushroom family. Their flavour is rich and intense – the very essence of mushroominess. Don't make this with dried porcini, which should only be used in sauces, stocks and braises. Use other wild mushrooms instead.

125 g butter

400 g fresh porcini, sliced, or other wild mushrooms, wiped clean and woody stem ends removed

3 garlic cloves, crushed

2 mozzarella, thinly sliced

3 sprigs of rosemary

salt and freshly ground black pepper

Pizza dough:

15 g fresh yeast

500 g *typo 00* flour

1 teaspoon salt

a pinch of sugar

fine semolina, for dusting

Makes 4 or 12 pizzette

1

To make the pizza dough, dissolve the yeast in 250 ml warm water. Pile the flour on a work surface and make a well in the centre. Add the yeast mixture, salt and sugar. Mix to a soft dough, then knead until silky and elastic. Dust with flour, put in a bowl, cover and leave in a warm place for about 1 hour until doubled in size.

2

To make the topping, heat the butter in a wide frying pan, add the sliced porcini and fry briefly on both sides. Stir in the garlic and seasoning and remove from the heat. Heat a lightly oiled, heavy baking sheet in the oven, set at its highest setting, until very hot.

3

Knock back the risen dough with your knuckles and divide into 4 or 12 pieces. Flatten each with a rolling pin and, using your fingers (or rolling pin), stretch into long flat oval shapes. Dust on both sides with semolina. Brush with the garlic butter, scatter with slices of mozzarella and top with the porcini and the leaves from the sprigs of rosemary. Arrange on the preheated baking sheet and bake at the same temperature for 10–15 minutes for large or 8 minutes for small.

Mushrooms, leaves and homemade crisps

This is the quintessential warm mushroom salad that can be knocked together in a matter of minutes. Homemade potato crisps make the salad special and they aren't difficult to make (though of course if you insist, you can use a packet of crinkle-cut store-bought crisps instead).

1

Using a mandoline slicer or food processor fitted with a slicing attachment, finely slice the potatoes. To achieve the cross-hatched line effect, use the serrated blade on the mandoline, set to fine slice, turning the potato 90° after each slice. Soak the potato slices in cold water for 30 minutes.

500 g mixed mushrooms

2 garlic cloves

leaves from 1 small bunch of flat leaf parsley, coarsely chopped

autumn salad leaves, such as baby red chard, baby spinach leaves and oak leaf lettuce

balsamic vinegar, to taste

salt and freshly ground black pepper

virgin olive oil, for frying and dressing

Homemade crisps:

3 large floury potatoes

oil, for deep-frying

2

Drain the potato slices and pat dry. Fill a wok one-third full of oil, or a deep-fryer to the recommended level. Heat the oil to 190°C (375°F), add the potatoes and deep-fry in batches until crisp and golden. Drain on crumpled kitchen paper.

3

Put the salad leaves in a bowl. Heat 4 tablespoons olive oil in a frying pan, add the mushrooms, garlic, salt and pepper and fry gently until the mushrooms are nicely browned. Stir in the parsley, then immediately tip the mushrooms and their oil over the leaves. Toss, season and sprinkle with balsamic vinegar. Serve with the crisps.

44

Serves 4

Mushroom and truffle mash lasagne

The lasagne can be prepared and cooked a few hours ahead – simply reheat for 20 minutes before serving. In fact it holds its shape and cuts better if it has been precooked. Truffle infused oil is vital for the success of this recipe. If you can't find fresh porcini make sure you add a few slices of dried porcini instead, but soak them first. I used a deep tin to make mine – it's fine to use your regular favourite lasagne dish instead, but remember to double up on the ingredients if yours is a big dish.

1 kg floury potatoes

100 ml single cream

50 g butter, plus extra for greasing

1 tablespoon truffle oil, plus extra for serving

2 tablespoons olive oil, for frying

250 g mixed wild or large cap mushrooms, sliced (include some porcini, fresh or dried)

10 lasagne pasta sheets, cooked according to packet instructions (don't use the bake-only variety)

120 g Taleggio cheese, thinly sliced

1 tablespoon milk, for brushing

sea salt and freshly ground black pepper

Serves 4–6

1

Cook the potatoes in salted water until soft, then mash with the cream, butter and truffle oil – this will produce a softer mash than normal. Taste and adjust the seasoning.

2

Heat the olive oil in a frying pan, add the mushrooms and sauté for about 3 minutes until just cooked and tinged brown at the edges. Season with salt and freshly ground black pepper.

3

Butter a deep tin or baking dish, approximately 18 x 12 cm. Place a layer of the cooked lasagne sheets over the bottom of the dish, cover with a layer of mushrooms, spread with a thick layer of mashed potato and cover this with thinly sliced cheese.

4

Repeat this process about 3 times or until you have used up all the potato mixture and have enough pasta and mushrooms left for one final layer. Arrange the remaining mushrooms across the top layer of pasta, moisten with milk, cover with foil and bake in a preheated oven at 180°C (350°F) Gas 4 for 40 minutes.

Variations:

• If you're feeling very rich, instead of mushrooms, shave paper-thin slices of white truffle over the top before serving, as in the photograph. At £2500 a kilo, this is obviously not an everyday practice!

Chicken and mushroom pie

Though spring is the season for morels, with their distinctive smoky flavour they are such an important culinary mushroom that I had to include them here. Dried morels are available all year round and, picked and dried in their prime, can be much better than many so-called 'fresh' ones.

500 g fresh, ready-made shortcrust pastry

90 g butter, softened

1 whole cooked chicken, about 1.5 kg

1 onion, quartered

2 garlic cloves

1 fresh bouquet garni of bay leaves, parsley and leek

3 blades mace or a pinch of powdered mace

500 ml good chicken stock

12 fresh morels, brushed clean, or 40 g dried (soaked in water until soft) or a mixture of wild mushrooms, including morels

1 tablespoon plain flour

60 ml double cream

1 egg, lightly beaten

salt and freshly ground black pepper

1 fresh chanterelle, to serve (optional)

Serves 4

1
Roll out the pastry to 5 mm thick. Spread 60 g butter over half of the pastry and fold the other half over the top. Repeat and fold twice more. Press together and chill for 30 minutes (this will make the pastry flaky).

2
Flake the chicken into chunks. Discard the skin and bones.

3
Put the onion, garlic, bouquet garni, mace and stock in a saucepan, bring to the boil, then simmer for 10 minutes. Boil until reduced by three-quarters. Strain and discard the solids.

4
Heat the remaining butter in a frying pan, add the morels and fry for 1–2 minutes. Add the flour and cook to a paste. Stir in the reduced stock and simmer to a thick sauce. Add the cream and the fried mushrooms and let boil for about 2 minutes. Taste and adjust the seasoning.

5
Roll out half the pastry and use to line an 18 cm greased pie tin or flan ring. Roll out the remaining pastry and slice into ribbons about 5 cm wide. Weave together. Fill the pastry case with the chicken and mushrooms. Pour in the cream sauce. Brush the top edge of the case with beaten egg and arrange the pastry weave on top. Trim the edges and then press together. Brush with beaten egg and bake in a preheated oven at 180°C (350°F) Gas 4 for 1 hour. Serve, topped with the fresh chanterelle, if using.

Pork chops with peppered wild mushroom gravy

No-nonsense pork chops with a rich autumnal mushroom gravy and a bowl of mash to mop it up – heart-warming stuff. Any mixture of wild funghi will do, including chanterelles and porcini, but you can also achieve good results with large open-cap mushrooms or smaller brown-capped chestnuts (slip in few slices of dried porcini to get the 'wild' flavour).

40 g butter

2 tablespoons olive oil

3 garlic cloves, finely chopped

1 large onion, chopped

3 bay leaves

3 tablespoons sherry vinegar

185 ml sherry or Madeira

20 g dried porcini, soaked in 150 ml hot water until soft

750 ml chicken stock

4 pork chops or loin steaks, trimmed of excess fat

350 g mixed wild and cultivated mushrooms

sea salt and freshly ground black pepper

creamy mashed potato, to serve (optional)

Serves 4

1

Heat half the butter and half the olive oil in a frying pan, add half the garlic, the onion, bay leaves and seasoning and sauté until the onion becomes transparent. Add the sherry vinegar and reduce until almost dry, then add the sherry, the porcini, their soaking water and the stock to the pan and simmer for 20 minutes or until reduced by half. Strain into a clean, wide saucepan and discard all the residue, including the porcini.

2

Heat a ridged stove-top grill pan or heavy-based frying pan until smoking hot. Rub the pork with salt, pepper and a little of the olive oil and char-grill for 4 minutes on each side.

3

Cut medium-sized mushrooms in half, trim off any woody stem tips and slice any large cap mushrooms. Heat the remaining oil and butter in the frying pan, add the mushrooms and the remaining garlic and sauté about 2 minutes or until tinged golden brown. Season, then add to the pan of gravy and reheat.

4

Serve the chops, mushroom gravy and mashed potato, if using, on preheated plates and sprinkle generously with pepper.

Apples are an easy fruit. Easy because they're easy to eat – there's no peeling (unless you're one of those fussy peel-all-fruit people) and, once they're picked, there's no waiting for them to ripen. They're easy on the tongue – crisp and refreshing, and easy on the eye – the most instant of instant packaged 'meals'. Sliced, sautéed, puréed and baked, they're a versatile and goodly lot.

I'm not a fan of whole baked apples – stuff them with whatever you like, there's no getting away from that blistering school pud: a scorched mouth and a mush of endless, rather bland apple. Apples need sugar – whole baked ones never seem to get the sweetness baked into them. Those I do love are small and full of flavour, and baked in caramel, as in tarte Tatin. (Yes please!) Or chopped up and baked into a pie with blackberries and lots of crumble on top. Or proper French glazed apple tarts – wafer-thin, tart yet sweet.

Apples have an affinity with butter, cream and alcohol – the apple-based Calvados and cider being obvious natural partners – while sugar sprinkled on top strengthens the apple's shape-holding properties. Apples don't, however, go well with other fruits, other than blackberries and dried fruits, but are wonderful with pork, game birds and cheese – especially salty and cream cheeses.

Granny Smith apples (a chance hybrid discovered last century by an Australian – yes, she was a grandmother, and her name was Smith) hold their shape well when cooking and are excellent for open tarts, as are Golden Delicious. I like Bramleys for pie fillings and purées – they contain higher acid levels and their flesh turns to foam under heat.

Some old varieties, of which there are several thousand, are now being reintroduced to our markets. They are aromatic and well worth trying, making a welcome change from the 'over-bred' disease-resistant supermarket varieties. Crab apples, the ancestor of our cultivated apple, are too sour to eat fresh, but make wonderful jelly for serving with pork or sausages.

In fact – apples are the perfect food. All you need is a wedge of mature cheese and one bottle of wine – and lunch is fixed. Easy.

apples

Apple duck confit
with masala baked beans

Duck confit is easy to make, but does require forethought. Make it in quantity, say 10 portions at a time – it will keep for at least a year in the fridge and you'll have it on hand for when you want an instant impressive dinner. It's as fast as a ready-made meal but miles ahead in flavour. If you don't want to make it yourself, buy canned duck confit from a good deli, or use roast duck with the masala beans instead – it's delicious too.

4 portions duck confit, store-bought or home-made*

1 onion, chopped

3 garlic cloves, crushed

3 cm fresh ginger

3 tablespoons vegetable oil, for frying

¼ teaspoon ground turmeric

3 teaspoons garam masala, freshly ground if possible

1 large Bramley cooking apple, peeled, cored and chopped

4 small whole red chillies

1 tablespoon sweet mango chutney

3 tomatoes, skinned and finely chopped

1 tablespoon sultanas

150 ml good chicken stock

500 g canned white haricot beans or butter beans, drained and rinsed

salt and freshly ground black pepper

Serves 4

1

Roast the duck portions in a preheated oven at 200°C (400°F) Gas 6 for 15–20 minutes or until golden.

2

Put the onion, garlic and ginger in a food processor and blend to a paste.

3

Heat the oil in a frying pan, add the onion mixture, the turmeric and 2 teaspoons of the garam masala and fry until browned. Season, add the chopped apple, chillies, mango chutney, tomatoes, sultanas, chicken stock and cooked beans and simmer until reduced and thickened, about 10–15 minutes.

4

Sprinkle with the remaining garam masala and divide between 4 heated bowls. Add 1 duck leg to each bowl and serve.

__Note:__ To prepare duck confit, trim the excess fat from 4 duck legs and arrange them in a shallow dish, skin side up. Sprinkle with 3 tablespoons salt, 3 sliced garlic cloves and crumble over a few dried bay leaves. Turn to coat, cover and chill for 2 days, turning once. Rinse the legs under cold water to remove the salt, then pat dry. Heat 1 kg lard or duck fat in a deep saucepan, add the duck legs and simmer very gently without frying for 1½ hours. Ladle a little of the fat into a deep, narrow container and, using tongs, place the cooked legs on top. Pour in the remaining fat until completely covered (do not include any of the meat juices at the bottom of the pan). Store in the refrigerator until needed.

Pot-roasted game bird

with apple, cabbage, juniper and cream

A cross between a roast and a stew, you can put this dish in the oven, set the timer, and forget about it. This method keeps the bird moist and tender so the meat will fall from the bones, just the way you want it.

1 game bird, such as pheasant
or guinea fowl, or a chicken, well seasoned

3 tablespoons olive oil

50 g butter

8 small pickling onions or shallots

2 garlic cloves, crushed

8 juniper berries, crushed

200 ml dry cider

150 ml good chicken stock

8 baby apples or 4 large, cored and quartered

greens such as the outer leaves of a
Savoy cabbage, red brussels tops or
black cabbage, separated into leaves,
thick ribs removed

150 ml double cream

salt and freshly ground black pepper

Serves 4

1

Heat the oil and half the butter in a large frying pan, add the bird and brown it on all sides. Transfer to a deep snug-fitting flameproof casserole.

2

Wipe the pan, then add the remaining butter, onions, garlic and juniper and sauté gently for 2 minutes. Pour in the cider and stock. Simmer for 5 minutes. Add the apples and transfer to the casserole.

3

Heat to simmering, cover with a lid, then transfer to a preheated oven and cook at 180ºC (350ºF) Gas 4 for 45 minutes.

4

Blanch the cabbage leaves in boiling water for 3 minutes, then tuck the leaves around the bird, pour over the cream, return to the oven and cook for a further 15 minutes.

5

Cut the bird into portions and serve with the apple, cabbage and juices. Other good accompaniments are sautéed potatoes and parsnip mash flavoured with truffle oil.

Apple griddle scones with blackberries

I first cooked this outdoors in a heavy pan over a wood fire with blackberries picked from the hedge – apple and berries are a delicious combination.

2–3 punnets blackberries

90 g caster sugar

2 small Bramley apples, peeled, cored and diced

110 g wholemeal flour

110 g self-raising flour

1 teaspoon baking powder

½ teaspoon mixed spice

110 g butter, softened, plus extra for frying

1 egg, beaten

1 tablespoon buttermilk

clotted cream or créme fraîche, to serve

Makes 2 large or 8 small

1

Put ½ punnet blackberries in a saucepan with 1 tablespoon sugar. Add 1 tablespoon water and heat until the fruit breaks down – about 10 minutes. Set aside.

2

Put the diced apple into a saucepan and cook until softened but still in chunks.

3

Mix the flours, baking powder, remaining sugar and spice in a bowl. Rub in the butter to make coarse crumbs. Mix in the apple, egg and buttermilk to make a wet dough.

4

Heat a heavy ovenproof frying pan, then smear with butter. Drop large spoonfuls of the mixture onto the pan and lightly flatten with your hand. If you wish to make perfect circles, place a cutter ring or flan ring in the pan first and press the mixture to fit the ring. Reduce the heat to low and cook for 10 minutes on each side for large scones and 4 minutes for small. Transfer to a preheated oven and bake at 180°C (350°F) Gas 4 for 5 minutes.

5

Put the scones on 4 small plates, cover with blackberries and juice, and serve with plenty of clotted cream or crème fraîche.

Baby apple pies

Pure unadulterated apple. No fancy flavours or hidden extras – apples can make it on their own. Cooked until silky smooth with a few little chunks for texture, then baked inside a buttery crumbly pastry, this is real comfort food.

375 g plain flour

185 g caster sugar, plus extra for dusting

185 g butter, softened

3 medium egg yolks

mascarpone cheese, to serve

Apple filling:

4 large Bramley cooking apples, peeled, cored and chopped

4 tablespoons caster sugar

juice of ½ lemon

Makes about 12

one 12-hole muffin tray

1

Put the flour in a large bowl, make a well in the centre and tip in the sugar. Add the butter and egg yolks. Using a fork, mash the yolks, butter and sugar together, then draw in the flour. Using your hands, mix well, then transfer to a work surface and knead well for about 30 seconds to form a smooth dough (Add a little extra flour if necessary, to form the right consistency. Wrap in clingfilm and chill for 20 minutes.

2

Put the chopped apple in a saucepan with the sugar, lemon juice and 2 tablespoons water and cook to a coarse purée, leaving a few lumps. Taste and add more sugar if you prefer. Cool, then chill.

3

Roll out the pastry to 5 mm thick. Using a biscuit cutter, stamp out 12 circles to line a mini 12-hole muffin sheet and 12 smaller circles for lids. Line the moulds with the larger circles of pastry and fill with the apple mixture. Brush the rim of the pastry with water, top with the smaller circles of pastry and gently press the edges together. Trim with a knife to make neat edges. Make 3 small neat holes in the top of each and dust with sugar.

4

Bake in a preheated oven at 190°C (375°F) Gas 5 for 20–25 minutes until golden at the edges. Let cool a little, then remove, dust with a little more sugar and serve with mascarpone.

Caramel syrup apples

with thick whipped cream

I love tarte Tatin – the soaked flaky pastry is good, but what makes it for me is the combination of melting apple saturated in caramel and all that extra buttery syrup that runs in rivulets into a pool of cream on the plate. So why not do just that. Forget about pastry, and have apples, buttery caramel and loads of cream. A seriously sensuous windfall in a bowl.

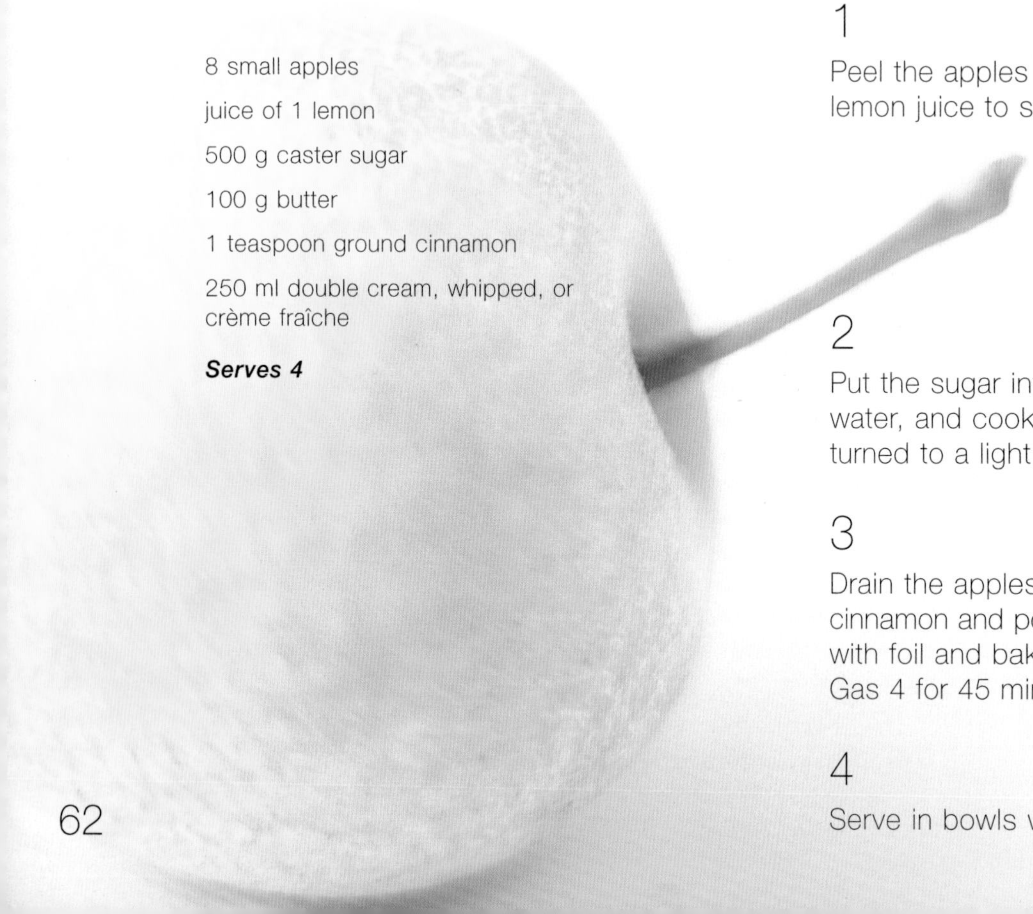

8 small apples

juice of 1 lemon

500 g caster sugar

100 g butter

1 teaspoon ground cinnamon

250 ml double cream, whipped, or crème fraîche

Serves 4

1

Peel the apples and put into a bowl of water mixed with lemon juice to stop them turning brown.

2

Put the sugar into a small saucepan with 1 tablespoon water, and cook over a gentle heat until golden and turned to a light caramel. Stir in the butter.

3

Drain the apples, pack into a deep dish, sprinkle with cinnamon and pour over the toffee caramel. Cover loosely with foil and bake in a preheated oven at 180°C (350°F) Gas 4 for 45 minutes or until the apples are very tender.

4

Serve in bowls with whipped cream or crème fraîche.

Sweet apple filo parchments

with goats' cheese, raisins and honey syrup

Apple with cheese and a sweet syrup may sound a little odd, but if you analyse the flavours – salt, sweet and sour – it isn't. I used Granny Smith apples because they hold their shape, but feel free to experiment.

2 Granny Smith apples, quartered, cored and finely sliced

90 g butter, melted

1 tablespoon caster sugar

2 tablespoons clear honey

1 tablespoon Calvados (optional)

4 sheets filo pastry

200 g goats' curd cheese or other soft cheese

2 tablespoons plump raisins (preferably muscatel)

icing sugar, for dusting

Makes 8

1

Toss the apples in 1 tablespoon of the melted butter and sprinkle with the sugar. Sear in a hot frying pan on both sides until lightly caramelized, about 2 minutes.

2

Dissolve the honey in 3 tablespoons of hot water, add the Calvados, if using, and pour over the apples in the pan. Simmer for about 1 minute, then decant the syrup into a serving bowl. Reserve the apples.

3

Cut each sheet of filo pastry into 4 rectangles. Brush half the sheets with melted butter and arrange the others on top, so you have 8 double layer rectangles.

4

Spread the centre of each with curd cheese, arrange a line of apples on top and dot with a few raisins. Fold the sides of the pastry over the filling – they look best if they don't quite cover – and brush all over with more melted butter. Put on a buttered baking sheet and cook in a preheated oven at 200°C (400°F) Gas 6 for about 20–25 minutes or until crisp. Dust with icing sugar and serve with the syrup for dipping.

Variations:

• Instead of apples, use apricots, dates or figs, sprinkled with chopped pistachios and add rosewater to the cooled syrup.
• Use mincemeat, soak the raisins in Calvados and add crumbled walnuts to the cheese.

A perfect pear standing on a perfect white plate is an image of total (affordable) elegance and refinement. From the Conference, with its russet-brown skin and elegant long neck, to classic pale yellow William or Bartlett and the portly Comice, each variety has its own character and shape. Their flesh is nectar-scented, buttery and pumped full of juice. Despite their sophistication, they don't allow for sophisticated eating. They're one of those fruits you just can't eat tidily: chin and fingers, and sometimes even arms, stream with juice.

A pear can't be man-handled – it's a temperamental creature. Choose fruit that feels firm, pack it carefully (don't sling it in your shopping basket) and eat it as soon as it ripens – it won't wait for you once it's peaked. If you leave it, it will turn 'sleepy' and although it may look appetizing, the flesh will have turned mealy, literally overnight. They're not as long-suffering as apples.

Most pears are sold refrigerated and unripe, so if serving pears uncooked make sure you buy them a couple of days ahead and leave them out in a warm kitchen to ripen. Most large pears are cooking pears but if you're going to poach them, any variety will do – you don't need to fret too much whether you've found the right one. Peeled and gently simmered in a syrup flavoured with vanilla, lemongrass, citrus, honey, wine or spice, the cooked flesh is like a fine osmotic sponge. They will absorb even more of the poaching liquid's flavour if left to bathe overnight, and pears poached in red wine can be left for up to a week (in the fridge) – the wine will soak right through to the core.

I think pears are best kept whole, cooked or uncooked – you can never chop up a pear, rearrange it and make it look better. Somehow you've just lost it. As a result, all my recipes in this final chapter use whole or halved fruit.

You don't want to cook? Then serve the perfect pear on the perfect white plate – with shavings of pecorino or Parmesan, or a wedge of creamy blue cheese. Simplicity is the key with this fruit.

pears

Chocolate pears

You can simplify this recipe to make straightforward chocolate-coated poached pears – no coring and stuffing. Poach them and then coat the pears with chocolate as detailed below. Serve with thick cream or mascarpone, or be creative and pack into a box (this one used to contain Christmas tree decorations).

2 tablespoons raisins

4 tablespoons rum

3 strips orange peel

120 g caster sugar

1 vanilla pod,
split lengthways

12 baby pears,
peeled and cored*

120 g white marzipan

250 g dark chocolate,
bitter or extra bitter, with
70 per cent cocoa solids

double cream or
mascarpone, to serve
(optional)

Serves 4

Note: *As you peel the
pears, put them in a
bowl of water with a
squeeze of lemon juice
to stop them going
brown.*

1

Put the raisins and rum in a bowl and leave to soak until plump.

2

Put the orange peel, sugar and vanilla pod in a wide shallow saucepan with 250 ml hot water. Bring to the boil and stir until the sugar dissolves. Add the pears and enough extra boiling water to cover the fruit. Poach at a gentle simmer until tender, about 10 minutes (depending on ripeness). Remove immediately from the poaching liquid and let cool on a wire rack.

3

Stuff the cavity in each pear with a little marzipan and a few rum-soaked raisins.

4

Melt the chocolate in a heatproof bowl set over a saucepan of simmering water. Do not let the water touch the bowl. Let the melted chocolate cool a little, then spoon it over each pear until completely coated. Stand on a wire rack to set, then serve and eat on the same day.

Pear tart with Catalan custard

I've used a thin, *crème-anglaise*-style custard flavoured with citrus peel, as the Spanish do to make *crème catalan*. If you like your custard thicker, add 2 teaspoons of cornflour with the eggs and sugar.

1 tablespoon lemon juice

4 unripe pears

1 vanilla pod, split lengthways

125 g caster sugar

250 g fresh, ready-made puff pastry

1 egg, lightly beaten

icing sugar, for dusting

Catalan custard:

300 ml milk

300 ml double cream

2 cinnamon sticks, broken

grated zest of ½ lemon

100 g caster sugar

6 egg yolks

Serves 4

1

Put the milk, cream, cinnamon and lemon in a saucepan and bring to the boil. Remove from the heat and set aside for 30 minutes.

2

Half fill a saucepan with water. Add the lemon juice. Peel the pears and put them straight into the pan to stop browning. Add the vanilla pod and sugar, bring to the boil and simmer for 25 minutes until just tender.

3

Roll out the pastry, 3–5 mm thick, and cut into long strips, big enough to fit 4 pear halves, side by side with about 1 cm between. Put on a greased baking sheet. Arrange the halved pears across the pastry and, with the tip of a knife, score a shallow cut in the pastry around each pear. Brush all over with beaten egg. Bake in a preheated oven at 200°C (400°F) Gas 6 for 20–30 minutes until puffed and golden.

4

Whisk the sugar and egg yolks together in a bowl. Strain the milk mixture and whisk into the egg mixture. Pour into a saucepan and heat gently, continuously stirring, until you have a thin custard that coats the back of the spoon (too much heat and the custard will curdle).

5

Dust the tart with icing sugar, slice into portions and serve with custard.

Espresso pears with mascarpone

Pudding and coffee served together – entertaining couldn't be easier. You can also flavour the coffee and pears with cloves, cinnamon or cardamom.

6 baby pears, peeled

500 ml fresh coffee (not instant)

3 tablespoons caster sugar

2 cinnamon sticks or 4 cloves (optional)

4 tablespoons coffee liqueur, such as Kahlua

mascarpone, to serve

cocoa powder, for dusting (optional)

Serves 6

1
Put the pears, coffee, sugar, spices (if using) and liqueur in a saucepan and simmer gently until the fruit is tender, about 10 minutes (depending on ripeness). Let cool in the liqueur coffee for 2 hours or overnight.

2
Reheat and serve hot, in coffee cups, with the mascarpone. Dust with cocoa powder, if using.

Variations:

• Add a square of dark chocolate to each cup, then fill with the liqueur coffee and poached pears.
• Put the pears and coffee into cappuccino cups and serve with hot frothy cream dusted with cocoa powder.

73

Honeyed vanilla pears with soft cheese

I used tall elegant Conference pears for this recipe, but any variety will do. If you want to make them look completely smooth and devoid of any lines left by the peeler, rub them all over with a tea towel after peeling.

4 Conference pears or 8 baby pears, peeled with a vegetable peeler

1 vanilla pod, split lengthways

4 tablespoons clear honey

3 tablespoons caster sugar

1 strip of orange peel

1 strip of lemon peel

juice of ½ lemon

robiola, ricotta or other soft cheese, to serve

Serves 4

1

Put the pears in a snug-fitting saucepan with enough water to cover. Scrape the seeds from the vanilla pod into the pan and add the pod itself. Add the honey, sugar, the orange and lemon peel and the lemon juice and bring to the boil.

2

Lower the heat, cover with a lid and gently poach for about 12 minutes for small pears, 20 minutes for larger, or until just cooked (test with a sharp knife, they should feel just firm in the centre). Let cool in the syrup.

3

Remove the pears with a slotted spoon. Heat the pan of syrup to a rapid boil and reduce until the syrup has thickened enough to coat the back of a spoon. Serve each pear with a slice or spoonful of cheese and the syrup poured over.

Variations:

• Use yoghurt cheese – mix 500 ml plain yoghurt with 1 teaspoon salt and suspend in muslin over a basin for 48 hours. The result will be a sharp-tasting cheese, excellent with the sweetness of the honey syrup. (You can also finely slice the citrus zest used in the syrup and mix this with the cheese).

74

Drunken pears with gorgonzola

You can't really beat a deliciously ripe nectar-scented pear with a salty piece of cheese. This is an embellished version, a good one for when the pears haven't ripened. The pears are best if left overnight – immersed in the wine juices, they become fully saturated with wine and spice.

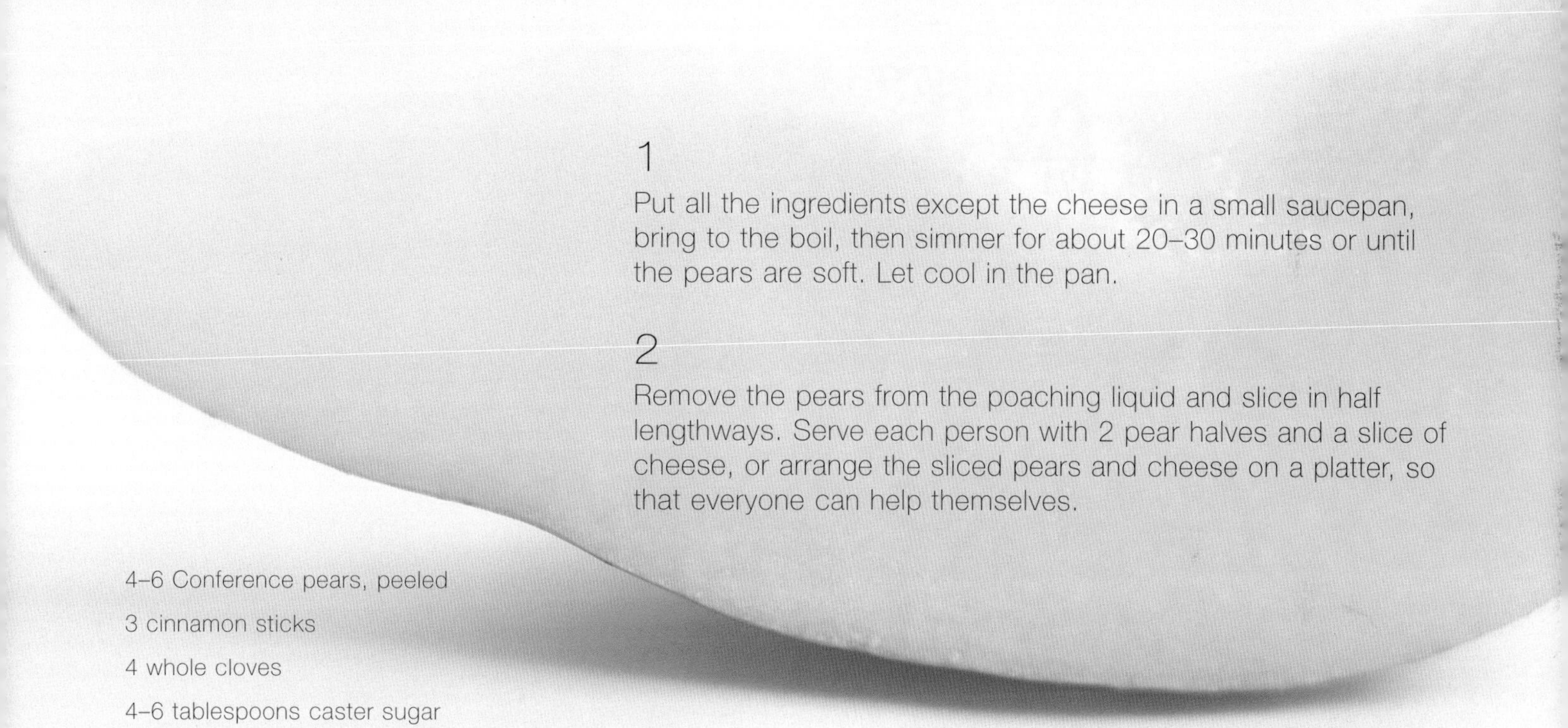

1
Put all the ingredients except the cheese in a small saucepan, bring to the boil, then simmer for about 20–30 minutes or until the pears are soft. Let cool in the pan.

2
Remove the pears from the poaching liquid and slice in half lengthways. Serve each person with 2 pear halves and a slice of cheese, or arrange the sliced pears and cheese on a platter, so that everyone can help themselves.

4–6 Conference pears, peeled

3 cinnamon sticks

4 whole cloves

4–6 tablespoons caster sugar

2 teaspoons allspice berries

2 teaspoons black peppercorns

2 bay leaves

1 bottle red wine (750 ml)

4 slices gorgonzola (portion size)

Serves 4–6

Variations:

• Serve halved ripe pears with broken chunks of Parmesan cheese, or on finely sliced Parma ham with a pile of chicory dressed with walnut oil, freshly squeezed orange juice and black pepper.

77

Ginger toffee pears with rice pudding

Rice pudding isn't just nursery food – it's rib-sticking good, as my grandfather used to say. Sometimes, a bit of plain honest home cooking is just what we need, but with these toffee pears, it's good enough for a dinner party.

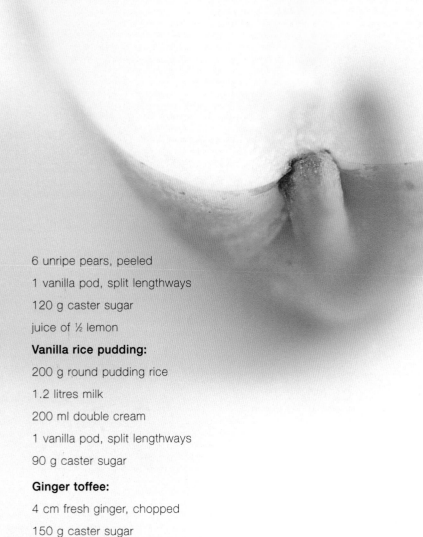

6 unripe pears, peeled

1 vanilla pod, split lengthways

120 g caster sugar

juice of ½ lemon

Vanilla rice pudding:

200 g round pudding rice

1.2 litres milk

200 ml double cream

1 vanilla pod, split lengthways

90 g caster sugar

Ginger toffee:

4 cm fresh ginger, chopped

150 g caster sugar

40 g unsalted butter

Serves 4

1

To make the rice pudding, pour boiling water over the rice and soak for 3 minutes. Drain, put into a saucepan, add the milk, vanilla pod and sugar and simmer gently for 30 minutes. Discard the pod, stir in the cream and spoon into a gratin dish. Cook in a preheated oven at 150°C (300°F) Gas 2 for 45 minutes.

2

To prepare the pears, put all the ingredients in a saucepan and cover with water. Simmer for 25–30 minutes or until tender. If not using immediately, let cool in the syrup. When ready to serve, remove from the syrup and heat through on top of the rice pudding.

3

To make the toffee, put the ginger, sugar and 2 tablespoons water into a small saucepan and heat gently until the mixture becomes a good caramel colour (watch it, as soon as it goes a deep red-amber colour, it's close to burning). Stir in the butter, then add 5 tablespoons water and stir well. Strain to remove the pieces of ginger. Pour some of the toffee over the pears, and serve the rest in a jug.

index

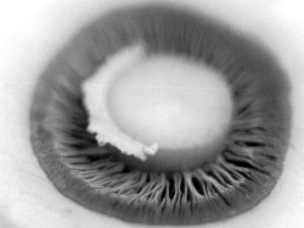

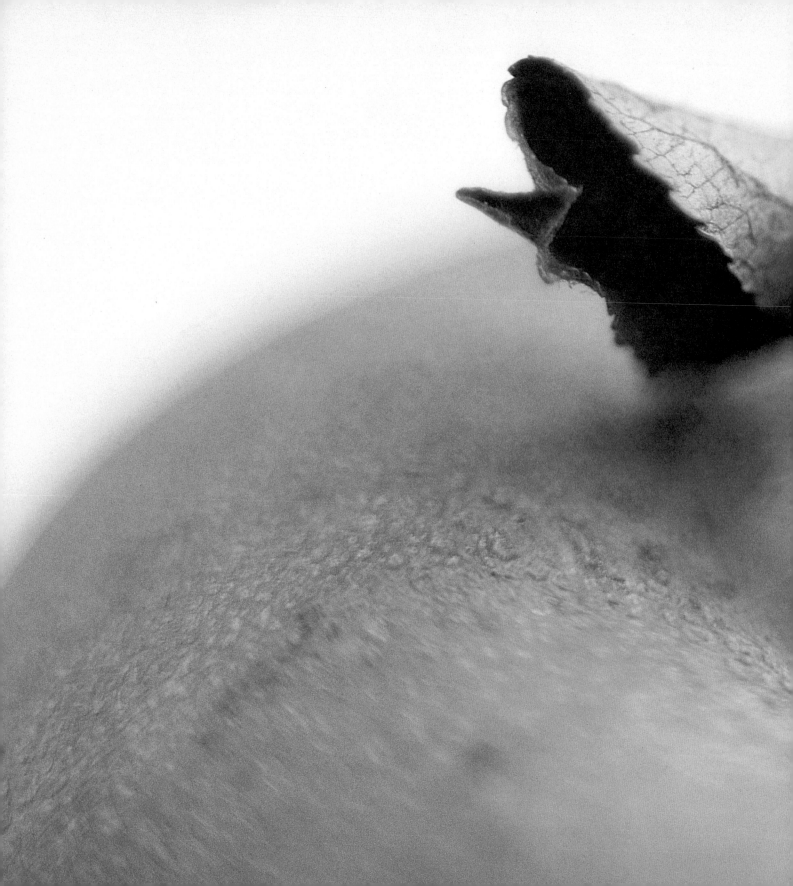

Goosey

A True Story

Patricia Iris Blaine

To order additional copies of this book, contact:
Xlibris Corporation
1-888-795-4274
www.Xlibris.com
Orders@Xlibris.com

Dedicated

To my dear husband, Jim,
who spent so much time helping me
take care of Goosey

Do you remember the story of Mary and her lamb which goes like this?

Mary had a little lamb
Whose fleece was white as snow
And everywhere that Mary went
Her lamb was sure to go

Well this is the story about Iris and her Coscoroba Swan, which goes like this:

Iris had a little swan
With feathers white as snow
And everywhere that Iris went
Her swan was sure to go

Goosey

Once upon a time, Iris and her husband, Jim, lived in Boston, Massachusetts, which if you look on the map, is away up north where it snows a lot and gets very cold in winter. So Iris and Jim decided to move south to Florida where it is sunny and warm. Their new home was on a lakeshore and all sorts of wildlife came to visit them.

There were herons, egrets, ibis, cranes, wood storks, cormorants, ducks and swans. And guess what lived in the lake? *If you said fish, you're right.* There were also turtles of all sizes that crawled out of the water to sun themselves. Cormorants swim under water, too, you know and like the turtles come out of the water to sun themselves and spread their wings to dry them.

It was fun for Iris and Jim to watch all of them, especially the birds. They discovered that they all ate bread except the herons and the egrets and do you know what they ate? *If you said sardines, you're right.* They not only ate them, they gobbled them up as Iris found out as she opened can after can for them.

One day a pair of Coscoroba swans appeared on the lake. They were much smaller than the other swans with red legs, red feet and red beaks but they had no *knobs* above their beaks. They were not friendly and would not eat anything either. In fact, they were so unlike other swans that Iris and Jim thought they were geese.

Soon after they arrived, the *cob* or *male* swan disappeared and before long the *pen or female* swan became friendlier and friendlier with Iris and Jim who thought it was because she was lonely. Anyway, she became their pet and, still thinking she was a goose, they named her "Goosey".

Goosey followed Iris everywhere: around the patio as she watered and tended her flowers and down to the lake where she fed bread to the fish and turtles. To her surprise, Goosey slid into the water and ate the wet bread right along with them. From then on, Iris kept a large bowl for water and cut-up bread on the patio so that Goosey could waddle up from the lake for a snack from time to time. With Iris and Jim taking turns feeding the birds and all their other animal kingdom friends, the backyard was a very busy place.

Although Florida is usually warm even in winter, something happened that first winter and the temperature dropped suddenly, reminding Iris and Jim of Boston. One night it fell to twenty-six degrees and stayed low for about a week. Goosey, who came from South America, didn't like that one bit. She began to have trouble getting around, standing first on one foot and then the other, as forlorn as she could be. Before long, she could barely walk.

Iris and Jim arranged the porch furniture so that they could lay a tarpaulin down just outside the sliding glass door. They then put an electric heating pad on the tarpaulin and on top of the heating pad a rug for poor Goosey to sit on. Goosey took advantage of their hospitality right away but she still looked sick.

Droopily, she sat on her heated rug on the porch and peered glumly through the sliding door at the large television in the family room. Iris moved the bowl of water and bread to within easy reach of her but Goosey ignored it and just sat there, staring listlessly at the television.

By now, quite worried about their pet, Iris and Jim called John, the person in charge of the neighborhood's Waterfowl Committee, who thought Goosey should be taken to a veterinarian. What does waterfowl mean? *If you said swans and ducks, you are right.* John then came right over with a cage to put Goosey in so he could take her to the veterinarian but Goosey didn't like the cage idea at all.

"Mac Magraw! Mac Magraw!" she cried, which is the sound she always made when she was upset.

Nevertheless, John put Goosey in the cage and took her to the veterinarian. It was then that John told Iris and Jim that Goosey was not a goose as they had thought but a Coscoroba swan. Since Goosey was a swan, the veterinarian prescribed some swan medicine to cure what he called her arthritis, Iris and Jim sprinkled the medicine over romaine lettuce as he suggested and waited. Goosey loved the lettuce and ate bunches of it which were sprinkled with the swan arthritis medicine but Goosey didn't get any better.

Meanwhile Jim, thinking Goosey might like a bed more natural than a tarpaulin, rug and a heating pad, got rid of them and brought her a bale of hay. He was right. She joyfully made a nest, then tucked the hay around her. Goosey began making soft clucking sounds, which is what she did when she was content. Then because she seemed to like television so much, Iris placed a small TV set they had on the floor of the family room next to the sliding door and left it on all night long. Goosey appeared to like commercials the best. *"That doesn't surprise me,"* Jim joked. *"Everyone knows that TV commercials are for the birds."*

However Goosey needed her daily swim but she couldn't walk down to the lake on her own without falling on her face. So it was up to Jim to carry her down to the lake for her swim and later, back to the porch. Then Iris got the bright idea of giving Goosey doses of her own arthritis medicine, which has always worked for her. After getting permission from John of the Waterfowl Committee, she started sprinkling glucosamine on the lettuce and before you could say *"Jack Robinson"*, Goosey was getting around on her own very well. She wouldn't go near the lake though without Iris and would not stay in the water unless Iris waited for her.

Then to make matters worse, two larger swans began to spend their time on the lawn between the patio and the lake, which scared Goosey and kept her from taking her daily swim. So Iris got her broom and walking ahead of her pet, made sweeping motions, back and forth, as though she was sweeping her lawn and the larger swans fluttered ahead of her down to the lakeside.

Goosey would then take her swim and splashed about as she cleaned feathers. But guess what? If *you said that Goosey would still not stay in the water unless Iris waited for her, you're right.* So Iris waited at the lakeside imagining that people passing by were saying, *"Why is that woman leaning on a broom by the side of the lake?"*

After a while though, Goosey, regaining her courage, went back and forth to the lake on her own. Then what do you think happened? *If you said two more big swans joined the other two, you're right.* Goosey was more afraid than ever.

But Iris, acting on the advice of John, got her umbrella and facing the four swans she shouted *"Shoo! Shoo!"* all the while opening and closing the umbrella as fast as she could which frightened them. The sight and noise of the fluttering umbrella drove them ahead of her down to the lake. This worked very well so Iris continued to do it and at the same time thinking that people passing by were now saying, *"What is that crazy woman with the umbrella up to?"*

Goosey once again regained her courage though, coming and going as she pleased and without her bodyguard, Iris. Although she spent more time away she still returned for a snack of water and bread that Iris kept on the patio and she also followed Iris around as she had before.

Now how do you think this story ends? *If you said happily you're right.* But not without other problems first.

Once in a while, Iris and Jim would take a trip and each time they would call John, the Waterfowl Committee man who would come by with his cage and take Goosey with him to his lake while they were gone. Each time Goosey would plant her self between Iris' feet and refuse to cooperate.

"Mac Macgraw! Mac Macgraw!" she would cry no matter what Iris did to console her.

However she would always make up with Iris and Jim when they returned. The last time was different though. When John brought Goosey back, she just sat on the porch and refused to eat. The next day Iris managed to coax her down to the lake for a swim and guess what happened when Iris returned to the house. *If you said Goosey disappeared, you 're right.*

When Iris called John to tell him, he told her that Goosey was sitting outside his back porch. What a surprise because John lived a mile or so away and had always driven Goosey to his place in the cage. But there she was sitting outside his porch which meant she had somehow made her way across the street and between houses and swam across a couple of other lakes to get there. *Wasn't she clever?*

Iris and Jim decided to leave her there because they thought she missed all the ducks at John's lake that were almost the same size as Goosey. Iris and Jim missed her very much though. Well, pretty soon an alligator came to that lake and because Goosey would be easy prey for the alligator as she moved so slowly, it was decided that she should be given to the Brevard Zoo for her own safety.

Because Coscoroba swans are so rarely found in the United States, it was very hard to find a mate for Goosey. But somehow the zoo, which had changed her name to *Suzie*, found one for her and they are both living in the zoo's South American exhibit where they will no doubt live happily ever after.

Coscoroba Swan

Range
Native of southernmost South America.

Habitat
Lakes, marshes, water, and land.

Size
Smallest of the swans.

Characteristics
White feathers with striking coral red legs and beak. Webbed feet.

Behavior
These birds have flapping flight and are unable to glide or soar extensively. They are flightless for some weeks after the breeding season, when flight feathers moult simultaneously.

More details at: http://www.xmission.comkhoglezoo/birds/coscoroba.htm

CPSIA information can be obtained
at www.ICGtesting.com
Printed in the USA
BVHW021614131221
623925BV00002B/20